Even So, This Song

Even So, This Song

LISA DART

SHANGANA PRESS

Published by
Shangana Press
Portland, Oregon, USA
shanganapress.com

ISBN: 979-8-9871359-2-1 (paperback)
ISBN: 979-8-9871359-3-8 (eBook)

Library of Congress Control Number: 2025941019

0 9 8 7 6 5 4 3 2

for
Peter Abbs
22 February 1942 – 6 December 2020

what restraint, limit
should there be to grief for one
so dear?
Horace

Contents

FAMILIARITY BREEDS CONTEMPT

So the saying goes. Not so.
The yellow paint of our kitchen walls
never fails to lift my mood.
Your deerstalker hat hanging
on one of the kitchen doors.
The shoes propped up
against the kitchen skirting board,
dusty from our last walk,
creased with the very
specifics of your tread,
unlaced in casual disarray,
wait, as always, for you to come,
lever your feet inside, pull the laces tight
to go to the park or somewhere new.
I loved looking at those shoes
on any trek we made, striding along
beside you. Always taking pleasure
in the rounded toe, the leathery blue.
(The last time, by your favourite river,
the ground dry dust for want of rain.)
The way you'd leave them,
scuffing our yellow kitchen walls,
the white skirting board,
sometimes made me rather cross.
There's no contempt in this familiarity.
Your death, so unexpected,
those shoes I cannot move.

A WINTER SO COLD

would be the reason

you woke

waking me as well

to slow motion

silent effusions

from a midnight dark

soft unending

tumbling flakes

a white confluence

in amber streetlight

and your awed reverence

"Oh beauty, beauty, beauty…"

another winter so cold

would be the reason

except that it wasn't:

high blood pressure,

furred arteries,

bronchial pneumonia

bronchial pneumonia,

furred arteries,

high blood pressure

not the winter so cold

though it was December

no tumbling flakes

in amber streetlight

nor your voice

in awed reverence

no *beauty, beauty...*

that other confluence

would be the reason

and now, for me,

a hard, unending

midnight dark.

JANUARY

A snow sky   few birds
silver birches spindled   loss
over rock cold stream rush

I LIVED BY TUNNELLING

My hands and feet clawing, scratching
and burrowing into the black-packed
earth of the past, piled up wounds
in clumpy, head-high mounds behind me.
I nosed forward, letting things
that happened go. But now, there's no dug out
muddy passage, nor any earthy heap. "He's dead,"
I go on saying, just as I said it *sotto voce*
to myself the morning I found you
in your red chair, snug in your navy dressing gown,
your eyes shut and, as always, a book
within arm's reach. Blinking in estranging light,
I couldn't grasp why you hadn't been to bed.
How could you have died? All the tunnels
I'd ever dug caved in. I couldn't even begin
to dig. The suffocating soil
of shock buried me alive.

I HAVE A PHOTOGRAPH IN MIND

Nothing could be more exuberant —
you're on the quayside in Mykonos,
the wind strong-blown, the sea behind
white-capped and, in the Greek sunlight,
the most soul-aching blue. You're waving
your summer hat defiantly, laughing, as the wind
billows your shirt and trousers. Such elemental energy
inspired you, and even dashed with sea-spray,
you're clearly having a great time. For days
I looked everywhere for this picture, desperate
to see you looking so happily alive. And in my dreams,
one, where I walk out to sea, another, on that quayside
where I've agreed to meet you by a fish restaurant,
it's you, you, not just that photograph, I cannot find.

THE PASSAGE BY OUR FLAT

A junkyard, even before you died:
old poles, bins, a rusted ladder,
seatless chair and troughs
you filled with soil for bulbs. Every
spring you carried them to our patio
so miniature daffodils nubbed
up green. No-one could be happier
than the two of us when daffodils
appeared. Yellows of joy, presence,
hope. Such delicacy. But the troughs
grew grass, tangled ivy, a snail-holed
sapling oak. I knew the passageway
had to be cleared. The rain, unremitting,
as hired men stooped and hauled. All
of it would go to the tip. A bulb
fell out. Once, your warm fingers
had pushed this bulb into expectant
earth. Hating the men, the rain, I
went inside. The bereft bulb
clenched in my hand. I buried
myself in your green bus coat.

ACT 5 SCENE 111

Wood boards. Not quite centre stage
Cordelia's body. Spot-lit.
Lear, on all fours
crawling around her,
sniffing at her corpse.
But for the shuffle
of his hands and knees,
the planetary silence. He,
a slow, demented wolf.
And who can tell how long it is
before his crawling ceases,
he throws back his head skywards,
time and space implode,
gravity strengthens ———
Howl. Howl. Howl.

FEBRUARY

Berwick church. Snowdrops
tremulous in winter wind
love-held shivering

PEVENSEY BAY

for Annabel Abbs

Yours, a daughter's grief: febrile fervour
to go, so early, to *his* places
and text me. I imagined pebbles,
those dark groynes, splintered,
rotten. Bladderwrack, the sun's yellow
washed out at dawn.

And the birds. Their high,
mystic flight, the yelping
ache of the unknowable
as if united, somehow,
with the dead. I couldn't move.
My grief, a limb-locked numbness.

Besides, there was only one journey
I longed to make. A mythic reversal,
where I am Eurydice, and he —
your father, my husband — Orpheus
strumming, as he always did,
his own lyrical music.

I'd take his hand without
looking round to see if he wore
his thick green bus coat, looped
orange scarf, broad blue shoes,
the brown fedora I'd bought,
and lead him from the underworld,
to walk along the shore with what
he loved most: you, me, gulls,
the sea's rhythmic plainsong,
sunlight's polyphony.

TRIBUTE TO YOUR LAPSED CATHOLICISM

There is a moment after you moved your eyes away.
The moment, say, after seeing Titian's life-size
The Crucifixion,
before exiting the sacistry,
at San Lorenzo de El Escorial Monastery.

I only glanced at your coffin — hard cardboard,
green leaves, cut-out paper hearts —
I had to look away. The moment
between, though infinitesimal, an infinity.

As if through some telescopic lens,
I could see your broad hands,
curved musculature, pale flesh,
untested dancer's feet, boy's smile,
those so intelligent blue eyes,
ribs which from the very first I loved.

As if I could hear a Stabat Mater to the sky.

MARCH

we cannot know from
tears the dimensions by which
the heart scales its loss

THE ONLY FAIRY TALE WE EVER READ

together, aloud, taking it in turns.
A winter afternoon, not much else
to do. Not a version either
of us knew. Though the story,
mostly, the one of childhood:
a woman, a monstrous creature,
sadness, recognition, love. How happiness
finally ensues. But we didn't know
the new prince would say to his princess:
"If you ever stop loving me, I will go
to the castle's lake, lay myself
down in the reeds." When you said
the same to me as if I, Beauty,
you, the Beast, my heart rent.
I made a silent, storybook vow: my love
for you will never cease. Beloved
Beast, after your so sudden death,
it is I, spell-broken, still laying
in the reeds. No-happy-ever
after happy. Wind, rain,
incessant bestial howling.

OUR HOME AFTER YOU DIED

Paintings on the walls. *At Motcombe Park*
with a pink swan and *Belle Tout,*
a lived-in lighthouse near Beachy Head.
We bought the painting when we'd just met.

And, though this is strange to say of sea,
the sky, somehow these blue tonalities
have your hands' tenderness. But, as is true
to memory, things in the painting are awry.

The lighthouse, too close to the precipice,
the gate, wrought-iron, rounded at the top,
shut against infinity. I skulk in and out
of rooms, imagine another painting,

called *Beachy Head*. A summer day
where the sea's white crescendos, painted
with a white-blue line, break to a sunned silence
far beneath the cliff's falling chalk, falling edge —

death for those who jump. But I'm taking
the light peach path to *Belle Tout's* gate, lifting
the latch, flinging the gate wide, running
through the sky, knowing I would find you.

APRIL

two smoke-grey herons
the rhizome of memories
wings on wind — birds gone

AT THE LOSS OF YOU

I'm thinking of that morning
the hard wrench

from bed
sky its head-strong self

the blue
too pristine

for my loping
from room to room

my home
dust-dead

the newborn sky
so life-opening

ended shock's
mute paralysis became

the scream
in my throat unleashing

wild-beast-wailing
from my stomach's deepest reach.

I FIND MYSELF UNMOORED

And ask everyone I know who lives alone
— an ocean so vast and deep for me —
how they navigate? Why aren't they adrift?

Emily Dickinson knew to *measure every grief...*
with analytic eyes; to wonder *if it weighs like mine,*
or has an easier size. No matter that I'm told:
you're your own woman, do whatever you like,
please yourself. Words, meant as ballast,
go quickly overboard, float like feathers.
There's no lifebelt. On uncharted, endless sea,
I lurch from side to side.

RETURN TO GERMANIKA, GREECE, WITHOUT YOU

When first I heard about her daughter,
and the compact white chapel with the blue dome, where,
not far below, the water laps beneath the pine tree grove —

When first I heard, I wondered how,
where tamarisk roots twist long and black down
the crumbling coastal path, any mother could come back —

When first I heard where, I did not know much
about death, nor the shut-off, shocked aftermath.
I knew Greek heat, goats, church bells, Homer's myth —

When I first heard, I imagined the hottest night, where
jasmine scent pervades the stillness of the perspicacious dark
and the sea, rhythmic, tidal, goes on and on, not like the heart —

All this, when I first heard. Now I, too, am back
and walk around that coastal path. Spring flowers – margaritas, statis,
poppies — make a wreath. You always swam in the place where

she fell, late at night breathing only shallow water. Alone,
I stand by the chapel now, where I have learnt that to return
allows love's valve to close and open up the cataclysmic grief.

AT THE BLUE HOUSE, GREECE

Your daughter took the mattress
downstairs for her son to sleep on

leaving the blue wood frame
empty. The base of pine slats

desolate in their disarray. That night
I dreamt I was talking to you,

planning a trip, laughing,
and, although the subtlest doubt

pulsed through the dream,
my heart-mind's

certainty: you were alive.
I woke to the day's breaking news:

two abandoned
pillows and the headboard's

thin line of worn paint,
where you always leant —

sitting up to write a poem
on your iPad, to read me

poems before I slept, or even
summer after summer

of the hottest sun, hardly able
to move, bear the thinnest

cotton sheet, just to drink
and rest. This news has no end,

a wordless loop
keeps playing and playing,

that rectangular cavern
next to me, which was once your bed.

FEAR OF NOT REMEMBERING

I want to fix something, hold it
firm, make it unforgettable.

Early evening in Paros, a clutch
of white, starred jasmine open,

cautious with their scent. I have
doubled over the blue wool,

handmade bedspread we bought
and always used to lay

across both our beds. April
has winter in the night air. But it's you

at our wild bay on Anti-Paros,
in blue crocs, light blue

swimming trunks, your blue towel
draped lap-long over one shoulder,

toga-like, a Roman sentinel
with a task no one understands,

sauntering along the water's edge —
the turquoise sea frothing white

through a metre of thick weed ——
skimming smooth white stones

after a cooling swim, I want. Want,
no matter what, forever in my mind.

MAY, YOUR FAVOURITE MONTH IN ENGLAND TOGETHER

and it is all here —
spring's lavish   doves   gold catkins
oh to tell you this

THERE'S SOMETHING OBVIOUS ABOUT PAIN

though its accoutrements surprise.
I remember that woman, years ago,
sitting opposite me on a train —
a summer when I had never been happier.
The day exposed by bare-flesh heat. The envelope
of her face white and flat, the flap
open wide, unstuck. She spoke,
gulping, "I've just lost my husband".

But there's something else more subtle,
almost philosophical in the absence
of a presence. It lingers
in the aletheia of material things —

I empty a wardrobe, fold shirts,
hang coat-hangers back. Widowed,
they dangle without purpose.
The leather belt's red lines
left on frayed, beige trousers.
The sandals that fell apart
in my hands. *Shoreline* written
in large letters on the inner sole,
and the black smudges
where once you put your feet.

OUR FIRST MAY TOGETHER

new growth on laurels
you picking ox-eyed daisies
"Viva la vida!"

THE COAT YOU WEAR IS
LONELINESS

Standing in the kitchen, hair
newly-cropped. The barber's razor
had been set on number one and you're
pleased to tell me this, detail not often
your strong point. Your hair shaved
so close, almost no hair at all, what we
called your *Michel Foucault*. Like his,
the fine shape of your skull exposed.
And then — so strange — we need a new
kitchen floor. I looked down at the pattern
in light wood, quite a bit of wear
and tear. I'd always rather loved
its lived-in look, but I still agreed.
For nearly two years now, you've
been dead. But in this dream, you put
on your big green bus coat, take
my hand, yours strong, though
not quite as warm, and walk me
through to the living room.

CHALLENGED TO RHYME

I am still at sea.
And rhyme predisposes me to prattle
or chant: *lagoon, moon, sand, dune*
as if a child stringing out a spell.

But the drone of the ferry that arm-in-arm
morning we went to Dieppe, the white birds
and cliffs as white as bone,
I remember well.

How can I rhyme?

You are dead. And death has the singularity
of stone. Come back,
take me away from this known world,
the blue of a lagoon, the yellow dune...

Rescue me from the far too familiar
dark sky, sorrowed moon.

THORNED

September. The rose hips red,
and their soft hanging
opens me.

At the swimming pool: the overwhelm of wet. Silked
  turquoise. Glisten.

In the jacuzzi, a man I didn't know kisses me. We'd hardly
  spoken. He just leant forward.
His lips determined.

I panic, my phone, small coffin,
not in my hand. I've forgotten to text you ——

the wound
of so-wanting you, absent.

In the day-eye of dreaming, the man dissolves.

I wake to the cold depth of death: I hadn't, seduced by blue water,
betrayed you.

Rose hips cut for what was once *our* table.
Thorned.
My hands bleeding.

YOU DESCRIBED THE HAWTHORNS ON BEACHY HEAD AS IDEOGRAMS*

blasted   leafless   gaunt   gnarled

extremities that disturb   deformity shaped

by grieving wind —— how the howls haunt

you called the hawthorns   ideograms of this wind

words your thing

I need   need your voice   calling out

through a hotel bathroom door   as you did once years ago

"words, words, my darlings, I love you!"   apropos

of what exactly   I'll never know

the hawthorn bushes

well-named   their clawing   spindled reach

      absence   *silence*

---

* Ideogram: A character symbolising the idea of a thing without indicating the sounds to say it.

MAY, AGAIN

what would you have loved?
today — the darkest lilac
white apple blossom

VIVA LA VIDA

I'm not going to let you become Miss Haversham
Anna Carlisle

Gladioli, the first living things
I brought into the front room
after your death and only then
because I didn't have space
in the kitchen. Three lots bunched
together for quick sale, the date
for selling overdue. Heavy, fibrous
green stalks and leaves, the flowers
not even opened. I lifted the jar
onto the bookcase behind a chair,
the room now, a grey-dust mausoleum.

I forgot about them.

But, after a few days stared in disbelief —
tall, elegant, poised for music, dance, song —
gladioli spilling flamboyance,
flamenco skirts of frilled crimson fire.

ASHBURNHAM PLACE

I am thinking of our last tea here,
in the Orangery, a winter day,
the camellias — were they still in flower?

Now, the heat, mediterranean,
silver birch trunks etched white
among abundant greens. The purple
reed tips feathered in the breeze. On
the lake's far side, swimmers' shouts
echo so many other years, other places.

And I long to make this poem better
than it is, with some philosophy
of grief knowing you'd approve.

Sitting here, trying to write,
I understand only how time,
casual with intimate company,
ignores me. Ignores the troubled
marriage between the immortality
of sky and death. Betrays all
of us with every summer's
seeming eternity —
the splash of sunlit water.

POETIC LICENSE
After Keats, for Alistair Davies

Autumn, still mild. No mists nor mellow
fruitfulness, but wind, rain ahead. We walked
to the seafront, to a bench, high, hidden
by bushes, fir trees. Sudden, above a hedge,
as if sprites, elfin eyes, smooth-skinned faces:
children peering at us and then, by magic, gone.
But they came back up the stone path. The bench,
their nan's beloved place. That day, the anniversary
of her death. No mature sun, no rose-hued
stubble-plains, barred-cloud-bloom. No swallows.
Ashen sky. A gull, the sea wan, and, far too near
the shore, a jutted line of darkling rock. One
mourner had a clutch of white freesias. The white,
stark and, with no brighter colours anywhere, all but
wailing. We left, fretful. Forlorn,
they sat on the bench to honour her.

Back at your house, we talked about a poem,
by Diane Seuss, 'Romantic Poet'. You found
the rhymes: *tits, pits,* coarse. Hated Keats
put down. My husband, a poet, nearly two years
dead, would have also loathed those rhymes,
the very words. He loved Keats, the rhythmical
music of the Odes. I liked Seuss's poem, wondrous,
understated, how it summons,
at the end, in just the final line, death
encoded in our bones but, even so, song:
the nightingale. Affirmation.
Full-throated grief.

33

TO KEEP GOING

Every day last summer I watered
and watered,
even the olive trees. In England,
in small patio pots, they become badly stunted. But the leaves,
green into silver, shook-foil shone
like the olive trees
on a patch of land in Greece. We were English, not Greek, but
The Dream of the Land.
The gate shone. The broken lock. Vines shone. Wild fennel,
        rosemary,
even the ants shone.
We dreamed and dreamed ——
most, and above all, wind-swayed
olive trees: green into silver, sun-shone.

Last summer's sun. Still, the Dream of the Land.
Beloved olive trees. Foiled shining.
My husband dead. A watering can.

PSYCHIATRIC WARD

four walls
around a white bath
stainless steel taps   subtle sentries

like: a comma   a colon
                    (semi or otherwise)
in a sentence

like: undecided hyphens   a dash   a word
            the exclamation mark's scream:
                        neck gash, wrist slash

voices crying: not for/for

spring and the scented hyacinths
rain   a child see-sawing   dust   the sun's heat
on the heart's rust   autumn's fettle:
blustered leafed griefs
winter's metal frost

voices crying: not for /for —

the cessation of time

terror of / desire for

            the end-stop line

HERE'S THIS WHEN YOU NEED ME MOST

is something I wish you'd said,
as you gave me the *This*
before you died.

Today, Easter Sunday morning,
the daffodils singing resurrection
from their deep-earth-sprung yellows,
I have to create the *This* myself.

Let it be a wonky, wrapped
package, (you decried your fingers, clumsy),
and, as on everything you gave me,
a label signed with a chiliad of kisses,
a squiggle meant to be a dolphin,
(your nickname for me)
and a sprig of rosemary.

Inside, with a leaf around it,
my present to you after we'd just met,
your silver and lapis lazuli ring
to remind me of all the every days,
you wore it.

This Easter Sunday,
the morning sky, the colour
of your eyes. And daffodils.

I rip the parcel open,
an inmate in an asylum.

THE AFTER

The knowledge,
slow seeping water,
she would have to change, begin again.

On her dream-mind's pure sky,
an indelible imprint. A bird,
heron-like, flying up, up, up,
vertical, without the use of wings.
Diamond-light clarity,
diamond-point intent.
And when the bird stopped,
she could only see its back.
Long wings held in close.
Long grey feathers, a feathered cloak.

A second bird flew to join the first,
such that they seemed one.
Until they parted, opening
as they did, grey shamanic wings ———

a third bird, smaller, emerged between them,
flew higher.

        A trinity.

The sky wordless clear.

She didn't know how to name the after.

Break: down/out/through.

EACH DAY

the severe lesson:
impermanence — the blossom,
this body, this breath...

THE SECOND AUTUMN AFTER YOUR DEATH

How it is still so easy,

to believe no-one's despair

is like my despair.

The calla lily that bloomed

last year and the year before —

white, carved with its own

statuesque significance, bought

and placed to remember you —

has grown only leaves. Huge ones.

Thrown into turbulence by the wind,

stomped by storm rain, this weather's

passing has left their stalks

unable to hold them up.

Quieted now, they're doubled over.

After the strenuous years

of *Just keep going,*

they too, their flowers gone,

in dishevelled grief. Today,

I wept again, longing

to talk poetry with you.

O forgive me this all-consuming,

still green ache.

DESCRIBING MADNESS

The five days she doesn't remember.

The belief she was moving out. Crockery smashed

or packed up. Pictures taken off the walls.

Candles lit, an incarnation ritual. Molten wax

pooled and, she didn't realise, solidified

as hard, white, unmapped lakes. The mind,

her mind unmapped, unhinged, undone,

unbalanced. Another *un* word: un-held?

That's part of it. The language.

The language. To say the rhythm's gone.

How to speak the mind's quiddity of distress?

A sheet rent from a straightened line,

flown skyward, an untethered breeze? What word

or words ever truly summon the thing itself?

The in-grown stress?

Take a lilac crocus. The lilac ones, her favourite

in the spring sun's iridescence. All that shimmer. Mere

outward appearance. Does a crocus

tremble in advance, prescient

its upright, flared splendour,

sanity of loved colour,

must collapse, strewn wayward?

And, does a crocus plead for its frail lilac light,

once extinguished,

to return again next year,

unashamed, undiminished?

NOMI'S DRAWING

Barren ground. Trees truncated.
Severed by the picture's edge. Her body's

a recumbent, desolate stretch
against another's. That body, compliant

stone. Blanket-wrapped. Smudged
shadow, ethereal lines

sketch-in the silence.
Her arm reaches across the chest,

her hand's grasp exaggerated,
a night-time commonplace

to lie this close before sleep, before the sun
draws back curtains, opens windows,

rouses another summer dawn.
Her coat hem stayed against her slippers

or are they boots? I can't quite tell
from the padded shapes.

Bowed down on the body's waist,
her hooded head. There's no sign

anywhere of movement. What to write
for this lightless, leafless,

faceless embrace?
Husband. Cold. Cannot. Dead.

THINGS WE SAY

I started painting the bookcase, but
stopped. The days, so hot.
I left books piled up high in the living room.
One day some of them toppled,
crashed down. I let them lie
there in disarray.

It is what it is, I thought.

I have mountained up
clothes on your side of the bed.
Our king-size duvet has stopped slipping.

It is what it is.

This cliché
stops the mind thinking.
Stops things, like the heart, unravelling.

The clothes' bulk: the sense
in deep-alone
sleep-space,
next to me
your presence.

The clothes
have the steepest, barren rockface.

SIBERIA AS DAY BREAKS

In the achromatic of an almost dawn
     a toboggan tugged by reindeers.
Balletic legs hold what seems impossible:
     their thick bodies bulked by thick, impacted fur.

The wordless white takes the eye to tone:
     black branch antlers, iron hooves,
          dark-ice cloud, the pewter of a not-now light.

And, as if in a narrative about grief, its vastness ——
     horizons frozen,
            bleak unending tundra ——
a hunched figure
        hunkered down,
is drawn
        into this morning's mourning candour:
a nascent shade of feeling
        somewhere between
the long grey lumbering
          snow,
            and slow sun-brim.

JUST MAY

Friston forest walk
splay of new lime-green beech leaves
rash of white bluebells

LAVENDER

I'm remembering your hands, broad and warm,
sculptor's hands you sometimes said, and how
between your fingertips, you'd crush lavender,
from any bush we passed. You'd always stop
and pick some, rub it in your palms, then smell
its long-reaching scent, which took you back —
it was her favourite — to your adoring mother.
Then you'd put your fingers under my nose
and I came to love the thin green stems,
the purple fragrant heads. I see you now
walking down our street, stopping, leaning,
picking the lavender that sways
against warm, orange brick.
Sun and birdsong auguring the summer.

AFTER MADNESS

It's taken years to understand
            childhood's artillery of colours:
the ones left behind
            for adult office,
                salaried suits, screens, paperwork,
believing
        whatever was wrong way back —
                father's suicide attempt,
the drugged, doll-eyed mannequin he'd become —
                  should be outgrown,
along with the primaries:
        play-school blue, nursery yellow,
            the primordial weaponry of Being,
                daubed for sky and sun.

But after madness,
        then trudging,
season after season,
        through disturbed, evening dark,
            too much heat, rainstorm's sudden tantrums,
to sound-out, to a therapist,
        the persecutory:
        guilt's flagellating voices,
self-hatred's monstrous shapes, loss, my mother's unintended neglect
        I've been returned to the young
            wax-crayoner of the celebratory,

that rapt adamant,
with brush, butcher's paper, smeared powder paint.

Now, I'm colouring with kaleidoscopic ammunition
puddled autumn leaves
— blush, corn, coral, lemon, mustard, turmeric, honeydew —
and those infant bullets of desire,
rose-hips' reddled beads.

DECEMBER 6TH

white peonies, bay
and holly from the oak woods —
in memoriam

LATE SEPTEMBER, EASTBOURNE SEA FRONT
for Nomi Rowe

The music of another summer's fading —
                    we talk of death,
        your husband's ashes, snowdrops,
                         apple trees in Normandy.

What matters now
        is the living after:
leaning out of grief
                into presence.
                        So we sing,
beneath the cathedral of the sky
                a hymn
to the immediate:
        blue Promenade railings, a dog, frenetic,
                by the waves' low fold,
the draw of the far-off headland,
        not quite navy, not yet turned to mauve.

From the Duke of Devonshire's statue,
                we saunter to the Grand Hotel,
a small-scale, flagged fortress,
                white for perpetuity.

Your face alert, our steps
                soft, intimate.
The sun warm, buttery,
                disavows the undertow
                        of Autumn.

And whatever we may, somewhere,
    still long for —— communion with *our* dead ——
this afternoon's harmonics,
      joys intoned,
         stall the inescapable:
            rain's threnody, the coming-in of cold.

THE SPEED OF THINGS

Things are so fast now, we find it hard to take them in, though
I'm not only talking broadband, breaking news, new builds.
Nor any picture, time or space, brought to screen on your
slick smartphone at running pace. I mean dreams. That come
from nowhere like the swans we saw once, driving on the
wooded road by a fast-stop Starbucks, the BP petrol station.
Above us the swans — emblems of power, purity, resonating
all that's beautiful, their wings, strong, startling our passing
through. But also, in those long, white necks stretched out,
a vulnerability, I didn't suspect. Something else, a frisson of
another time, a far-off place. As we drove, the swans soon
lost to us, the mid-January sun became a globe of liquid light
between the trees, a huge orange scintillate intent on hide-
and-seek. And, that evening, the Wolf moon. Wolves, I'm
told, don't exactly howl at the moon — their howling's to
communicate: danger, stay away or desire, here I am. Their
faces, moon-turned, for the clearest sound. And, somewhere
out in the snow-drifted, snow-scudded cold, the things inside
I can't put to time: that winter sun, those high-sky swans,
wolves' howls, your death, — all oscillates in my mind, never
gone. The wolf-moon too, blood-red, still with me, though it
disappeared as I slept. When I woke, something else always
there, echoing, took its place. Not an in-transit orange
silhouette, nor howls bayed out long in cool moon-bright,
but something (and only present for a moment's grace) in
the not-yet-eclipsed dream I'd had — that sunlit, snow-swan
image of your face.

MARCH

Sunlit wayward grass
lilac crocuses singing
grey heron swoops in

MY IMMENSE HAPPINESS

day-to-day, your voice, saying
my nickname 'Dolphin'.

The willow tree, a mourning
cloak draped over the grey lake.

But wait, the rousing
breeze through the willow's green leaves,
a sojourner's whisper, Latinised
the way you did only for my ears, our togetherness:

Dolphinissimus, Dolphinissimus, Dolphinissimus . . .

DEAREST LOVE, THE DAFFODILS HAVE COME

Tall, public ones. Miniatures too! Shy. Intimate
with that wondrous
tender glance
you sometimes have.

I'm on the train to Lewes. How often we've made this journey
    together...
Trees steeled with frost.
Bare wintered land.
The station flower shop is selling tête-à-têtes
snug in strong brown paper. I'll buy some on the way back. And,
I know you know this —
I am just saying it, walking to the town centre —
I'll leave them at the top of the stairs.
We've done this ever since you moved in, haven't we?
Always. Well, more than twenty years, something
on the landing: flowers, fruit, a card left
for whichever one of us would be last home.

On my way back now, the poetry meeting good.
You'd have liked all today's poems.
Frost holds up the air's bright cheer.
The sky's blue arc, seductive.
Gulls: blown white kisses,
these scribbled pages signed, *Much Love.*
The train shunts on —

trees splay light.
Their steel, perfidious.
On the edge of a field, a deer
crouches in the cold.

I do know you're dead.
Really I do.

And that, even though I've bought some,
there's no need, on the stair top, for daffodils.

ACKNOWLEDGMENTS AND APPRECIATIONS

Each of you listed (alphabetically) below know, as I do, the ways you supported me, encouraged me, hugged me and walked with me, often along the sea front during the Covid shutdown, after the death of my husband. My huge fortune: the unique ways — staying in the house with me, making funeral arrangements, writing obituaries, haikus, soups, walks, postcards, meals, books, phone calls, DVDs, daily texts, chocolate, flowers and more — how you all helped to stitch the quilt of life together again and wrapped me in.

You kept me holding on to life, kept the poetic spirit alive in me and kept me writing.

I am more than immensely grateful to:

Cleo Abbs; Theo, Kerry, Angela, and Ailish Abbs; Colin Bell; Patrick Bond; Julian, Linda, and Robert Broughton; Nigel and Dawn Butler; Anna Carlisle; Liza Catan; Sara Caton; Sally Collins; Kerrie Curzon; Alistair Davies; Mark Divall; Miranda, Stewart, Sam, and Callum Ferguson; Andrea Hollander; Craig Jordan-Baker; Kim Lasky; Silvia Macrae-Brown; Paul Matthews; Martin Merson; Jane Mogford; Lorna Pidgeon; Nomi Rowe; Ruth Sibson; Stella Skordalellesis; Annabel, Matthew, Imogen, Bryony, Saskia, and Hugo Streets; Kay Syrad; Teena Wallis; Ann Williams; Patricia Wooldridge; and Lynne Wycherley.

Specifically regarding the poems in this volume, particular thanks go to Paulann Petersen, who, after a very thoughtful and careful reading, creatively suggested *Even So, This Song* as a much better title than the one I had come up with. And, great thanks, too, to Andrea Hollander, Patricia Wooldridge, Kim Lasky, Kay Syrad and Ann Wroe for reading the final manuscript and giving it their generous endorsements.

Finally, a huge thank you to Gemma Whelan and Adam Liberman of Shangana Press for deciding to publish my work. Adam, thank you too, for everything you have done preparing the manuscript.

DEDICATIONS

'I Have a Photograph in Mind' is for Theo Abbs.

'Pevensey Bay' is for Annabel Abbs.

'Returning to Germanika, Greece, Without You' is for Miranda Ferguson.

'Ashburnham Place' is for Kim Lasky.

'Poetic License' is for Alistair Davies.

'To Keep Going' is for Jane Mogford.

'Just May' is for Silvia Macrae-Brown and Mark Divall.

'Late September, Eastbourne Sea Front' is for Nomi Rowe.

PREVIOUS PUBLICATIONS

'The Speed of Things' was first published in *Unbroken* (Issue 21, 2019) https://unbrokenjournal.com.

ABOUT THE AUTHOR

Lisa Dart is a poet and prose writer. A finalist for the Grolier Poetry Prize (USA, 2004), The Aesthetica Poetry Competition (UK, 2013), and The Troubadour International Poetry Prize (UK, 2022), she has a doctorate in creative writing from the University of Sussex (UK). Her poetry has appeared in many journals, including *Eastern Iowa Review*, *Tears in The Fence*, and *The London Magazine*. She is the author of *The Linguistics of Light* (poems, Salt, 2008); *Fathom* (prose memoir, Free Association Press, 2019); *This Thing of Darkness* (IPBooks, 2024), a highly experimental illustrated book using multiple texts, which won a British Arts Council Award; and *The Bird You Are* (Shangana Press, 2025).